THE FIELD REPORT

Jenni Field
Redefining Communications

Jenni Field has almost 20 years' experience in communications. She specialises in helping organisations go from chaos to calm; working to help them understand how to get teams to work together better and operations work more efficiently. She is an expert in ensuring alignment between communication and the business strategy. Before setting up Redefining Communications Jenni worked as a Communications Director for a global pharmaceutical business and, prior to that, she was Global Head of Communications for a FTSE 250 hospitality business. Jenni has experience working in defence, retail and hospitality sectors as well as not-for-profit organisations. It is this experience that has contributed to the development of The Field Model™ and Jenni's book, *Influential Internal Communication*.

CONTENTS

Welcome to *The Field Report*, a combination of my thinking: From leadership and culture to hybrid working and mental resilience, there are lots of topics affecting organisations.

A lot of these require time to think and *The Field Report* has been compiled to provide some opinions to get you thinking, as well as offer practical tips and advice to help you make changes.

I want you to be inspired so for each section you'll find a "Be Inspired" page where you can find recommendations for TV shows, books and podcasts to keep you entertained and thinking differently about work.

Hopefully this is also a useful reference book for you. Something that you can refer to in the future to help you shape your business strategy, leadership development programme and internal communication plans.

As always, it's about continuing the conversation, so you'll find details at the back to connect with me and the broader Redefining Communications team.

Let's look forward, at the possibilities that are ahead for organisations around the world to do things differently, to be more human and to put communication at the heart of the workplace.

Thank you for reading.

Jenni

Jenni Field Founder, Redefining Communications

HYBRID WORKING

According to ACAS, "Hybrid working is a type of flexible working where an employee splits their time between the workplace and working remotely."

BBC Worklife, on the other hand, says, "Hybrid work tends to include more freedom around when to work as well as where... Ideally the best of both worlds: structure and sociability, and independence and flexibility."

I like the second definition, because it's wider: it's not about location, it's about culture.

Is the focus on hybrid working a distraction for leaders?

Location agnostic, hybrid workforce – just two terms being used to describe how the world of the work is changing.

Since the pandemic hit there has been lots of chatter around the workplace, getting back to the office, and how it will work with some people at home and some in the physical office location.

In 2020 we saw the likes of Twitter, Facebook and Square declare that employees will never have to return to the office, and discussions turned to the purpose of offices, why we need them and whether we will need them again.

In 2021, a more balanced approach emerged. Salesforce shared their categories for workers to choose how they want to work and Google announced workers would return to the office. Hubspot also said that one of their goals for 2021 was to have 70% of job roles location agnostic.

There are two things to look at here – the purpose of the office, and how people want to work.

There have been a lot of people stepping forward who have worked remotely for years, sharing their advice and guidance on how to do it successfully. But working remotely and working as a truly flexible organisation is very different.

The knowledge worker vs the frontline worker is now a very different world and friction between the two groups has been a challenge for organisations since the second half of 2020 – and it is continuing.

But all of this has brought me to the conclusion that hybrid is a bit of a distraction for leaders. I don't think we should be focused on hybrid working and how to operate a hybrid business.

The ability to work anywhere has been the case for years. Maybe not embraced by all but it's not completely new. It's also not an option for a large population of the workforce (deskless or frontline workers). I think we need to look at the bigger picture.

"Wherever work happens" is an important phrase because, for years, work has been happening on trains, planes, in cars, coffee shops and more. Freelancers who chose to break away from the constraints of office life have worked in cars outside piano lessons, next to hospital beds, etc. Work has not been confined to an office for years. Not since the use of technology that has enabled such a shift to the way work gets done.

So rather than getting caught up in the latest buzzword of hybrid organisations, can we focus instead of the need for flexibility. Flexibility that reflects the reality of life today. A way of working that engenders trust and operates on an adult-to-adult basis. Now is the time to focus on the output of the work, not where and when it is being done.

This is about a fundamental shift in what we see as the working day in society. It's about having the ability to focus on our priorities. To focus on what's important with balance and boundaries. To accept that what works for me might not work for you and that's ok.

HOW FEAR AND CULTURE WILL IMPACT HYBRID WORKING

The divisive nature of some of the messaging about hybrid working is likely to cause a serious organisational divide. This started during the first lockdown for many in the UK – the divide in organisations where there is a split between frontline and knowledge or office-based workers. The comparison between a comfortable working day at home vs the risks of being frontline was discussed at length.

Fast forward a year and the conversation isn't going anywhere. But alongside it, we now have very real dialogue about working in different locations, commuting and our personal levels of comfort about that risk – all linked to fear. The fear we feel related to the impact of COVID-19 and the fear we were possibly being made to feel through stories in the media and those shared by our networks on social channels. But the thing about fear is that it stops us from moving forward. It stops us being able to make changes that could potentially be brilliant for society and work.

· ·

"Let me assert my firm belief that the only thing we have to fear is fear itself – nameless, unreasoning, unjustified terror which paralyses needed efforts to convert retreat into advance"

President Roosevelt

This shift and potential divide is one piece of a complex puzzle that requires a fundamental shift in terms of work and society. For organisations, this is simply culture change. But what we are focusing on is categorising employees and talking about booking systems for desks. This is the soft, easy stuff.

We aren't talking about the big stuff – the things that require behaviour change or the conversations that allow us to explore "how things get done around here" in a post-pandemic world with more flexible working practices.

We know that culture change takes time. Hybrid working isn't a quick fix. It isn't a "let's be hybrid for a few months" or "let's create a project about hybrid working". Because if you were to change organisational culture like that, without really thinking about what it is that needs to shift and what that looks like – actually, tangibly looks like – then it probably wouldn't last long.

There is a lot to consider about work. There is a lot to be mindful of in terms of individual circumstances. Paul Zaks' concept of "Freedom in a Framework" is your friend. Let's not put rigid structures around something that requires inherent flexibility, and let's approach this like any culture change strategy – and please, give it the investment of time it needs to succeed.

Dig into the data

75%

Pre-COVID-19 75.8% of businesses
asked had an office occupancy
of roughly 81%

Pre-COVID-19 36.2% had no
remote workers, 33.2% had
only 1 – 9% remote workers

20%–60%

Post-COVID-19 they're
expecting office attendance
to be between 20% – 60%

50%

Sept 2020 66.4% said
50% of their workforce
was now remote

*Source: Will hybrid working ever work research by
Management Today partnered with Hays in September 2020*

50%+

Post-COVID-19 21.8% expect 50% or more to stay working remotely

75%

75% of employers believe they'll have to mandate the return of employees to some degree

50%

50.9% of businesses didn't think there was any difference in employee productivity compared to the same time in 2019

55%

55.1% of businesses thought their employees were just as motivated as they were in 2019

THE PANDEMIC REVOLUTION AND WHAT WE CAN LEARN FROM OUR HISTORY

It's going to take us 25 years to reap the true benefits of flexible working... that's if the Industrial Revolution is anything to go by. I've coined the term, "pandemic revolution" to explain the opportunity that's in front of us.

Inspired by reading Matthew Syed's book *Rebel Ideas* where he talks about what happened in the Industrial Revolution linked to innovation, we can see how we're likely to miss the opportunity in front of us. His link of the Industrial Revolution to innovation is my link to the pandemic and how we are focusing on the wrong things.

In *Rebel Ideas*, Syed says:

"Electricity... offered huge dividends: not just in terms of power but in the redesign of the manufacturing process...In a traditional factory, machines were positioned around water and, later, the steam engine. They clustered in this way out of necessity. The production process was umbilically linked to the sole source of power, with the various machines connected via an elaborate, but often unreliable, set of pulleys, gears and crankshafts..."

· ·

*"Electrification meant manufacturing could break
free of these constraints… machines could have their
own source of power, allowing the layout of factories
to be based around the most efficient workflow
of materials. Instead of a single unit of power
(the steam engine), electricity permitted 'group power'."*

But this didn't happen:

· ·

*"Instead of streamlining factories…they
dumped a large electric motor in the middle…
as if a substitute steam engine….they completely –
almost inexplicably – missed the point. This would
prove catastrophic. The economist Shaw Livermore
found more than 40% of industrial trusts formed
between 1888 and 1905 had failed by the early 1930s."*

On top of this failure, there was also an impact on the pace
of the Industrial Revolution:

· ·

*"… electrification in the late 19th century meant
electrical motors could replace the older, less efficient
steam engines. It created a second surge in growth and
productivity, the consequences of which we are still
living with today. Except for one thing. This surge was
curiously delayed. It didn't happen instantly, it seemed
to pause… for around 25 years before taking off."*

During the Industrial Revolution, the technology and opportunity were there but we replaced the old with the new without thinking about the broader constructs around us. For me, hybrid working is being talked about in exactly this way.

We need a more flexible approach; recognising that work is not the same as it was years ago and that technology has changed what we do for many. Not only this, but life is different. The balance and flexibility needed by everyone when there's no longer a "work until you're 60 and retire" mentality requires a different approach to work, and a shift from the division between work and home. Adding to this, the globalisation seen in recent years means the concept of out-of-hours work is archaic.

This doesn't mean we blur all our time or that we don't need to put boundaries in place. It does mean we need to think differently about it all. We shouldn't try and change one component which, due to the pandemic, seems to be location. We need to look at society and work as one and stop trying to separate the two in the same way we've done for years.

We're focusing the conversation on being in the office and how to communicate with each other when people are located in different places. We're discussing what this means for meetings and working together as a team – but it's not about that.

The pandemic revolution can only happen if we look at things as one. This makes it a bigger, more uncomfortable conversation, but it's the one we need to have.

We can move into hybrid working practices, but this has to be interim. It must be while we have these conversations and there has to be action that follows them.

THE SKILLS WE NEED TO TAKE US INTO THE NEXT ERA OF ORGANISATIONAL ENGAGEMENT

The Bionic Business report from Simply Communicate published at the end of 2020 provides insight into the way organisations need to change to adapt to a hybrid working environment in the wake of the COVID-19 pandemic. A bionic business balances digital and physical workspaces in such a way that it enjoys positive employee engagement alongside strong, sustained business performance.

The report outlines three key characteristics of what a bionic organisation is:

— They go beyond simple empathy, and everyone is united behind a common purpose, so much so they feel personally involved in the business
— They're proactive in communicating change – actively encourage new, collaborative behaviours
— They have stepped beyond the first wave and are exploring automation of repetitive processes and looking at AI.

This made me think. For years we have seen barriers for internal communicators remain the same – the challenge with deskless workers and line managers as a conduit for information.

In addition, we have seen skills in PR static – the desired skills or the skills gaps around research and evaluation, business acumen and project management aren't new.

This means that when it comes to making changes for a hybrid world, we need to invest in skills and areas that have needed attention for a long time:

Impactful communication training: helping people realise how their communication style impacts others. If we want to have an organisation that goes beyond empathy, we have to start with making sure that empathy exists.

Resilience training: if we're looking to embrace change and adapt behaviours then we need to make sure people have the skills to do that. Change isn't easy for humans, so making sure that we're aware of the impact it has on us and how to keep on going when it feels challenging are important skills to develop.

Psychological safety: this needs to underpin everything inside an organisation in order to enable change, innovation and collaboration. There cannot be proactive encouragement without safety in place.

AI, tech and automation in the workplace: we have to understand how this can work, what the impact is on processes, people and more. If we don't invest in upskilling ourselves in this area, we cannot support the organisation's desire to move to bionic.

. . . .

The reports tells us that market research from IDC predicts that by 2023, 75% of organisations will have comprehensive technology roadmaps, up from 27% in 2020. That is a huge increase so we need to invest in ourselves to make sure we know enough to advise those around us.

For years we focused on the nine to five, the rush hour and the physical office. All of that has now changed. Industry articles highlight that flexible working, work/life balance, the importance of emotional intelligence and resilience are all areas where work has changed. How we learn at work, the reskilling needed, and health and wellbeing are all a focus that will carry forward into the future.

So when it comes to creating a bionic business we have to consider whether the people in the organisation have the right skills to support and advise such a change – are we really ready to work in a hybrid world?

And if we aren't, now is the time to invest in ensuring we will be sooner rather than later.

*Be Inspired

There is so much content out there about hybrid working. From podcasts to books about remote work, there is a lot to explore. So much of the content links to good leadership, regardless of location.

If you like to read, *Remote Work* by Chris Dyer and Kim Shepherd is a good starting point. Another one that has been recommended is *The Long-Distance Leader* by Kevin Eikenberry and Wayne Turmel.

If podcasts are your thing check out my podcast, *Redefining Communications with Jenni Field.* In the very first episode I discuss how we need to think differently about work.

If you want to explore some of the broader considerations around the Industrial Revolution and how this can link to work and innovation – Matthew Syed's book *Rebel Ideas* is excellent.

HANDY HINTS

Five steps to making hybrid work for the long term

How do we embrace hybrid working and ensure our organisations are fit for the future? We can do this using elements of The Field Model™ and the three phases of understand, diagnose and fix. But it's going to take time, conversations and the acceptance that things need to change for everyone at work; not just the office worker.

1. Understand the symptoms and what they mean

We must start with the symptoms that teams are experiencing today. Mainly because they have been here long before the pandemic. The challenges people have around juggling childcare/ other family care and work is one. The need to be able to swap shifts if things come up is another. There has been a challenge for years with people not being given the ability to manage their *work* time around their *whole* time – the symptoms we see are burnout, unhappiness, low retention rates and more.

2. Diagnose what this means for your organisation

Every person, every team and every organisation is different. We cannot standardise how to operate even by industry because there are too many variables. We might talk about organisations and how they work but organisations are people – they don't exist without them and they're all very different. So, we have to take time to work out what people actually need and want from life and work – together. What would make things easier? What makes things difficult? Does the shift pattern work or does it need to change? Can people job share? Will they be in the office or working from home?

3. Diagnose what this means for how you get things done

Diagnosis must include business processes. And because processes require communication, it all falls under the changes that can be made when we work smarter together. What are the options to get the work done? If we currently do it like this, could we do it like that? You have to be challenged to think differently, especially if this is how it has always been.

4. Give everyone a voice

This doesn't mean you can't create something that works for everyone – think "Freedom in a Framework". Give people the chance to share their ideas and what they need. Make sure you obtain this information without a bias on hierarchy, team or individual. Listen. We have spent a year talking about the need to be more human at work – now is the time to demonstrate what that actually looks like.

5. Fix how you work for a flexible future

The fix has to be about changing how work gets done and changing how people work together. This will include the hours people work, especially for those that are office based. If it's more convenient for me to work 6:00 am to 8:00 am and then 10:00 am to 2:00 pm, then that's ok. It's about getting the work done, not the time at a desk. If the meeting is in person and I have no others that day, I can come in for the meeting and then go home. An office can become a place to get together and collaborate and nothing more.

LINE MANAGERS NEED INVESTMENT, EMPOWERMENT AND AUTONOMY TO THRIVE

For years, the role of the line manager has been something of a mystery. For those working in internal communication, the line manager is sometimes seen as a barrier to effective communication throughout an organisation.

We all need an anchor point in our organisation. Something we tether to. This could be a person or a location, but it's about having a point of connection.

Are line managers an anchor point? Do we need line managers? What is their role today? I teamed up with research and data experts, SocialOptic, to explore these questions.

Research: Line managers under the microscope

We really need to understand from line managers themselves what it is they do so we can appreciate and enhance their role for the benefit of the organisation.

My previous research into the role of the deskless worker told us that the line manager is the most important person for those disconnected from the organisation. We needed to ask line managers about their role and how it needs to change inside organisations.

In May 2021 our Line of Sight report was published after line managers from lots of different industries completed the survey to tell us more about their role.

Here are the top six things to take away from the research:

1 More experienced managers know their weaknesses

- More experienced managers are more likely to tell you they need help with their communication skills. They also feel less confident in training their teams to communicate effectively.
- New managers struggle with putting time into building relationships and managing conflict.

2 Self-awareness is low when it comes to communication skills

- We know that 17% of remote workers thought their manager was not a good communicator when we asked them in the *Remotely Interested?* research. In this research we asked about capability and 80% said their team would say their skills were good – this is a big gap!

3 Line managers aren't listening

- Managers who don't get regular feedback are less effective at retaining their teams.
- Those who never get feedback state they are communicating effectively, but how can they know this?

4 Not all line managers are the same

- We group them as line managers but many have very different roles. There is a difference between managing a few people in an office to managing 20 people who are all on the road. The skills needed, the ability to connect – they are all different.

5 Empowerment vs autonomy

- 98% manage people but only 50% manage budget and resources. This means that line managers have control over the people side of their team but not a lot else. This makes us question whether line managers are empowered or whether they are autonomous?

6 Matrix management has an impact on happiness

- When a line manager reports into matrix management they are not as happy or as engaged as a manager who reports to one person. This is important because for many organisations matrix management is the norm and it is having an impact on teams all the way through the hierarchy.

EMPOWERED DECISION MAKING IS NOT DECISION MAKING AT ALL

As we saw in our Line of Sight research, line managers may be empowered, but the autonomy to lead and manage is non-existent without budget and resource responsibility.

When it comes to the different approaches to management and culture, many leaders have moved on from command and control. This top-down approach has its place in organisations where leaders prefer to be the authority figure – the ultimate decision-makers. The problem is that this rigid approach doesn't allow team members to develop management or leadership qualities and it keeps working relationships in parent-child mode.

We're more likely today to hear leaders talk about "empowerment" and "autonomy" among teams: adult to adult. However, the distinction between empowerment and autonomy is important when it comes to exploring how people adapt being back in the workplace, and imperative to know when it comes to trust and integrity.

Autonomy is different from empowerment. When it comes to organisations being in chaos, the disconnect between decision-making and management can often come up. For the line manager, the inability to make any decisions that will benefit the team or make a difference is paralysing.

> "
>
> *Autonomy is the freedom to act and to make our own choices. Empowerment is the granting of political, social or economic power.*

Gustavo Razzetti, culture design strategist

It stops progress. It's inefficient. It supports hierarchical power inside organisations.

It's easy to give someone the power to make the decisions you want them to make. It's less comfortable to give people the freedom to act based on what is in the best interests of their stakeholders. "Freedom in a Framework" is something to aim for.

HANDY HINTS

What the Line of Sight research tells us to do next:
- We need to look at several factors to improve the role of the line manager. This needs to include organisational design, communication and training
- The culture around empowerment and autonomy needs to be discussed with the leadership team to be clear about what it is the organisation is actually doing
- Look at the role matrix management plays inside your organisation and whether it works
- Internal communication teams need to look at the quality, relevance and timeliness of their content for line managers
- Invest in line manager skills in communication – they might be great at the tasks and the job but skills to lead and manage people are different.

These are the three things to consider when it comes to the skills of the line manager:

Make time
Make time for your team, really listen to them and help them overcome challenges (put your phone away, take notes, prep for the meeting). Recognise their achievements and work with them to help them achieve their own goals and aspirations.

If you don't know how, ask for help
You can often be promoted to manager because you're really good at the tasks involved in the job. It's likely there's been little training in how to manage and even less exposure to the importance of communication in that relationship. If you don't know how to manage or have questions, ask for help. This isn't a weakness, it is a necessity to be able to be help coach, mentor and lead in what you do.

Be accountable and make others accountable
Make sure that what you say and do are the same. Being aware of any gap and its impact can really change relationships and cultures in the workplace. If you say you'll be at a meeting at 10, be at the meeting at 10. Consistent behaviour builds trust and enhances individual credibility.

MENTAL RESILIENCE AND ADAPTING TO CHANGE

Mental
Of or relating to the mind.

Resilience
The power or ability of a material to return to its original form, position, etc, after being bent, compressed, or stretched. The ability of a person to adjust to or recover readily from illness, adversity, major life changes. The ability of a system or organisation to respond to or recover readily from a crisis, disruptive process.

Mind over matter

There is a difference between mental health and mental resilience.

Mental health is about our emotional, psychological, and social well-being, and can affect around one in four people every year.

Anyone suffering chronic mental health problems should always speak to a medical professional. Workplace mental resilience interventions are not recommended for those either off work with or returning from mental health-related problems.

I like to think of mental resilience training as preparatory work, enabling you to better handle life's setbacks. Think of it like this; if you put your raincoat on before going out in the rain, you're more likely to stay dry! It's also about understanding that it will rain some days – and it'll be OK.

Knowing how to be mentally resilient better prepares you for knockdowns, and gives you the skills to get back up again.

Mental resilience v. mental toughness?

Research indicates subtle differences between these two; most suggest mental toughness is resilience plus confidence. We have heard the differences described as:

Resilience: *a defensive strategy to help you get back up when you have been pushed down.*

Toughness: *an offensive strategy that may prevent you from getting knocked down in the first place.*

We advise avoiding 'mental toughness' as a term, as it can conjure up images of physically demanding experiences, e.g. rowing the Atlantic or operating in war zones.

Traits of mentally resilient people – some of us are born with it but we can all build it:
- Viewing change as a challenge or opportunity
- Commitment
- Recognition of limits to control
- Engaging the support of others
- Close, secure attachment to others
- Personal or collective goals
- Self-efficacy
- Strengthening effect of stress
- Past successes
- Realistic sense of control/having choices
- Sense of humour
- Action-oriented approach
- Patience
- Tolerance of negative affect
- Adaptability to change
- Optimism
- Faith.

Source: Conner and Davidson (2003)

MENTAL RESILIENCE AT WORK

In the workplace, a lack of mental resilience can manifest itself in many ways. Everybody is built differently. For example, one person may be a whizz when it comes to delivering presentations, whereas another could go into a flat spin merely at the thought of it.

On the other hand, some are open to criticism of their work, take it on board, and strive to make the appropriate improvements, seeing the criticism as an opportunity to learn and grow. Others get embarrassed and frustrated. They take it personally and resentment forms, causing friction between them and their line manager.

Learning how to be resilient should bring balance to your skill set and reduce situational stress levels. Training can be delivered to help people learn appropriate coping strategies. If delivered well, this training should improve both workplace output and the individuals' mental wellbeing.

Different resilience levels can impact the workplace

Low-level resilience:
1. Fears change
2. Fearful of management
3. Struggles to complete tasks
4. Rigid
5. Distracted
6. Requires constant guidance
7. Often needs extra support
8. Appears self-absorbed
9. Pessimistic
10. Reactive
11. Feels most things are too hard
12. Constant feeling of guilt / pessimism

High-level resilience:
1. Open to change
2. Good comms; asks for help or clarification
3. Perseverance to see task thorough
4. Adaptable
5. Good problem solver
6. High levels of initiative
7. Supportive
8. Sees bigger picture
9. Confident
10. Proactive
11. Can-do attitude
12. Cheerful

Line managers and leaders

For teams to be successful it's important they feel part of something. Not just the organisation, but a close-knit band of people who have shared values and purpose.

They need to be able to rely on each other and look out for one another. This will allow for more positive adaptations to change and to respond to setbacks effectively.

At Redefining Communications, we created the model **TEEAM** to help foster and maintain team resilience. In our workshops we encourage line managers and leaders to consider how effectively teams are working together:

TIME

Take the time to understand and get to know each other. Part of building mental resilience is about awareness of ourselves and the impact we have on others. We need good relationships in the workplace for the organisation to thrive.

EXPERIENCE

We can often learn from each. Think about the experiences you've had that have boosted your mental resilience and how you could pass on knowledge to your team. Sharing experiences can help you pull together during difficult times.

ENCOURAGE

Support and encourage each other; celebrations and rewards are important. Recognising the big and the small wins is an incredibly powerful tool in building team resilience. The benefit of taking time to get to know your team is that you'll understand individual requirements for recognition.

ACTION

Look at goals and the steps you are taking to do what you say you will. Don't let the say-do gap become an issue within your teams in a way that impacts trust. Knowing you can rely on each other is essential in building resilient teams.

MONITOR

Keep an eye out for any signs of stress or burnout within your team. Look out for breaks in resilience, which may manifest itself through challenging relationships. Make sure key team members aren't shouldering all the burdens or carrying others who are either less experienced or less able. Checking in regularly can build helpful social connections that are a key element of resilience.

Resilience and leadership – the attribute everyone needs to build

Amy Modglin (CEO – Modglin Leadership Solutions) wrote an article for *Forbes: Why Resilience Is Necessary As A Leader.* Here is what she had to say about the importance of resilience in leadership:

. . . .

With every struggle comes a tremendous opportunity. These are the times where you can choose to embrace the gift of adversity and use it to strengthen your leadership abilities. Your chance to show your integrity and your ability to work through the hardest of times.

It is your responsibility to lead through good and bad times. Good times are a reason to celebrate and reward people. However, nothing is more rewarding than coming out of a storm as a stronger leader and a more cohesive team.

Your actions during a crisis serve as a model for your followers. Remember, as a leader, your people are watching you all the time. The way you compose yourself serves as a model for those around you.

Learn from your failures. Adverse times are a great teacher. If you carefully evaluate every mistake, every failure, every obstacle, you will uncover a lesson that will be important for you to learn from to become a more resilient leader.

"

Each of us is unique! Therefore, it stands to reason that we are all born with genetic differences. These differences determine our individual ability to how we physically react to stressful situations.

As we are most likely to face stressful situations in our adult life, we have, probably without realising, built up various strategies to help us cope.

Training and experience (experiential learning) provide us with most of the tools we need to build resilience. Sometimes though it needs somebody else to unlock your potential, just like a personal trainer does for gym-goers or business coaches do for leadership teams.

John Humphreys, mental resilience trainer with 25 years' experience in the British Army.

*Be Inspired

There is tons of content in books, films and TV series relating to mental resilience. Almost all good stories, both in books and on the screen, involve the protagonist's world being turned upside down followed by an escalation of events; then finally change that leads to the resolution to the problem.

A good starting point would be *The Queen's Gambit* on Netflix – a story of a young girl overcoming adversity in order to succeed. Mariana Bockarova, Ph.D. wrote an interesting article for *Psychology Today* discussing how the series ties in with resilience research.

As far as non-fiction work goes, anything related to stoicism is worth a read, but these can be heavy reads so try YouTube for a summary if you are short on time. Two suggested titles are:

– *The Obstacle Is The Way* – Ryan Holiday
– *Meditations* – Marcus Aurelius

Outside of typical theories of stoicism other options to look at are:

– *The Art of Resilience* – Ross Edgley
– *Life Under Fire* – Jason Fox

Next time you're watching a film, TV series, or reading a book, see if you can spot the patterns mentioned above. You may find inspiration in their story.

MENTAL RESILIENCE AND HOW IT HELPS IN A CRISIS

You will have noticed that 2020/21 was probably the hardest year we have witnessed in recent history; perhaps since the Second World War. In particular, 2020 was a very openly divisive year; with topics such as Brexit, the Presidential election, Black Lives Matter, mask-wearing, and conspiracy theories dividing workplace and family opinions.

Add to that confusing advice and statistics regarding the COVID-19 pandemic, vaccination programmes, missed education and home schooling, employment uncertainty, and lack of social interaction. It's no surprise that it was tough. Overall, it's been a time of arguments and unknowns, leaving many of us living in a constant state of anxiety.

In the UK, 2021 continued with a national lockdown. There were ongoing uncertainties about Brexit, despite a last minute trade agreement with the EU. And we're still unsure of how the economy will recover, when the vaccination roll out and booster programmes will complete, or if they'll remain successful. Many people hoped that 2021 wouldn't be as bad as 2020. The truth is, it wasn't. There's so much still out of our control, but not everything.

By working on our mental resilience, we can at least learn how to prepare emotionally for what lies ahead.

There are a few techniques you can start to use to help you and, in a crisis, they come in very handy. Understanding control is one that we always share in our resilience training workshops;

> **Control:**
> Controlling your environment is important. You control how you spend your time and energy and sometimes we can forget that.
>
> You cannot do everything and therefore you have to edit your choices based on what you want to do. Author, Matt Haig talks about editing choices in his book *Notes on a Nervous Planet* where he states that we cannot possibly watch every film or read every book. So, you have to edit things out and spend time doing things that help you achieve your goals.
>
> You can also control how you respond to things. Always ask yourself if you can control or influence a situation – if you cannot do either, let it go.

Boundaries in a blurred world

The physical boundaries between work and home have gone for many so how do we set them? How do we make time for ourselves? I have been asked these questions many times.

The answer is a firm talking to and it links to resilience!

You have to be firm about the boundaries you are putting in place and they have to be realistic. If you know your rhythm is now working later then make sure you start work later. Don't just extend your day. Change your pattern. Start work at 11:00 am and finish at 7:00 pm. Create a working day around that timeframe making sure you start and stop at those times.

It is easy to find excuses not to: "I'll just get this done."
"I'll do it now so I don't have to do it tomorrow."

Don't listen to that voice. Stop. It's a discipline that you just need to embrace and practice. It is doable!

· ·

Years ago, I would start work at 6:16 am on the train and get home at 7:30 pm. I ate lunch at my desk and often missed the gym because of work.

This had to change so I told my boss I was doing 8:00 am – 4:00 pm. I am an early bird, so mornings are my friend. Walking out the office at 4:00 pm felt alien. I felt naughty. I was full of shame as I scurried out. But, day after day, this got easier. If there was something urgent, I was contactable, but I was heading home and going to the gym.

The lesson? Nothing bad happens. I didn't get fired. I didn't stop delivering my work. I had time for me. I was healthier. There were no negatives. We fear the unknown because we are hardwired to fear it. But taking the step is the first move forward.

The important thing here is to tell people this is your pattern. It's a conversation with your team or manager to ask for meetings to start a bit later to help you manage your time and workload. Sure, there is compromise and this might not be daily, but have the conversation and test it out. You might find you'll have to change things again in a few months too.

Find your new rhythm. Make it a conversation with those around you. Prioritise what is helpful not harmful. Be firm with yourself to stick to the boundaries that are right for you.

ADAPTING TO CHANGE

"You need to get comfortable with ambiguity" was what my old boss told me. I really struggled with this, partly because ambiguity was everywhere, and nothing seemed to make sense: from the strategic narrative to the organisational structure.

Since I had this conversation, I have read and researched more into how we work as human beings. My book, *Influential Internal Communication*, features a whole chapter dedicated to understanding people because, I believe, it's fundamentally important for us to understand each other to enable better working relationships.

One of the main things I talk about when I speak about communication in the workplace is how we work as human beings. Specifically, how we are designed to dislike ambiguity. How we have to be able to predict what is happening to stay safe and how we make up stories when we don't know.

Over time, my research and learning has continued in various areas and, during the pandemic, it has been around resilience. There is a clear link between building mental resilience and communication, which is why I now have an expert in my team (John Humphreys) and offer workshops to help teams explore this.

As my reading and research continues, the link between ambiguity and resilience is even clearer. When it comes to "getting comfortable with ambiguity", what can we take from the traits of resilient people to enable us to be OK with change?

Adaptability: be more like a tree. A tree will bend in the wind, it will flow with its surroundings. Likewise, water will flow around a rock, it won't just stop.

Given my nature to fix things (and the very essence of The Field Model™), being adaptable is key. There is always a way forward and there is always a solution, it's just about discovering it. You have to find that way around the rock and you have to let your surroundings guide you so that you can move forward, even if it feels more sideways at the time.

Humour: things aren't always funny, but you can see the funny side of things. Most people I know will comment on how I am always smiling. I'm genuinely a very smiley person and it's rare that I'll go a day without laughing.

However, I do take what I do seriously, and I know the impact it has on individuals, teams, and organisations: but that doesn't mean I can't have fun while I do it. I've been caught in the wheel of seriousness before and it wasn't healthy for me – as my friend and fellow Calm Edged Rebel, Advita Patel, often quotes for those in communications and PR, "we work in PR not ER!"

Hopeful equanimity: optimism is not always the best approach. It can be unhelpful and can have devastating consequences if it isn't grounded in realism. Cue hopeful equanimity.

I came across this when I was reading Ross Edgley's book, *The Art of Resilience*. There is a story in there that stayed with me and one that I shared with my community:

Admiral James Stockdale had a coping strategy
while in a Vietnamese prisoner of war camp:

. . . .

*"I never lost faith in the end of the story. I never
doubted, not only that I would get out, but that I
would prevail in the end and turn the experience
into the defining experience of my life, which in
retrospect I would not trade.*

*Optimists will say 'we are going to be out by
Christmas' and then 'we are going to be out
by Easter'. The optimists in the camp died."*

Stockdale says:

. . . .

*"You must never confuse faith that you will prevail
in the end (which you can never afford to lose)
with the discipline to confront the most brutal facts
of your current reality, whatever they may be."*

In other words, have faith, but don't tie the hope to
an external circumstance that you can't control.

Stockdale was firm in his hopeful equanimity rather than
optimism. Equanimity is calmness and composure, especially
in a difficult situation. It's about having the balance of hope
and optimism with realism.

We aren't designed to be OK with ambiguity. We are designed
to ensure we are safe and that nothing will cause us harm.
Ambiguous situations make us uncomfortable because we

can't predict what's going to happen and as a result we cannot be kept "safe".

But we can take steps to build our resilience, and this will allow us to take that edge off. Steps that will give us the confidence to keep moving forward and not be paralysed by the fear of the unknown.

Being human – keeping an eye out for burnout and the seven ways to solve your stress cycle

From the second century AD to 2021, humans have suffered loneliness and the pandemic has intensified this. The series of lockdowns created sustained levels of underlying stress that our bodies weren't used to or designed to cope with. It's a dangerous combination that can lead to burnout.

Mental resilience connects to our ability to face challenges and stress positively. We all have individual levels of mental resilience but when it's low, it can lead to burnout.

A key element of building your mental resilience is finding ways to manage your stress cycle to reduce burnout, which is generally defined by three components (Freudenberger, 1975):

1. Emotional exhaustion: from carrying too much for too long – when we are stuck in an emotion rather than moving through it. This is most strongly linked to negative impacts on health, relationships and work.
2. Decreased sense of accomplishment: a sense of futility or that nothing makes a difference.
3. Depersonalisation: depletion of empathy, care and compassion.

In a Brené Brown podcast, Brené discusses burnout with Emily and Amelia Nagoski, co-authors of *Burnout – Solve Your Stress Cycle*. They identify some incredible insights and advice: and I loved the specific advice about **the seven best ways to end the stress cycle:**

1. Physical activity: this, they say, is the "first line of attack" and can be anything from walking, dancing, weightlifting or yoga.
2. Breathing exercises: take big, slow deep breaths – try breathing in for four, holding for four and breathing out for six – over 90 seconds. This engages your parasympathetic nervous system by regulating the central nervous system.
3. Positive social interaction: building a connection with people gives a homely feeling of safety.
4. Laughter: not polite laughter, but the kind of snorting, proper belly laughter! The argument for injecting some humour into our stress is summarised brilliantly (and humorously) in a TED Talk by Loretta LaRoche, *How to Humour Your Stress*.
5. Affection: a 20-second hug can change your hormones, lower your blood pressure and improve your mood.
6. Have a big cry: learn to set what's upsetting you aside and focus on the physical sensation of crying, without feeding why you're crying in the first place – see it through to its conclusion.
7. Creative expression: arts and crafts, sketching, DIY or knitting – the act of making something allows you to channel feelings into something positive and tangible. It allows your imagination time to be free.

We're not alone in feeling lonely

Loneliness can be a major form of stress and impacts productivity and efficiency. A study published in the *Harvard Business Review (America's Loneliest Workers)* found workers are less satisfied with their jobs, receive fewer promotions, switched jobs more frequently and are more likely to quit their current job.

The study also stressed that managers need to be aware that some people are more prone to loneliness than others, such as single and childless people, those with fewer people in their private life and those who identify as anything other than heterosexual.

I can't help thinking that tackling loneliness and finding innovative ways to connect remotely, will be a central part for organisations in the future. Creating connection and belonging in a hybrid or remote world will require intentional activities and a focus on organisational culture.

We need to become better at spotting the (subtle) signs both in ourselves, and in a colleague or employee, such as social withdrawal, reduced productivity, poor work quality, lower levels of energy and negative thinking.

What can we do to combat loneliness?
- Create opportunities for meaning
- Find times to check-in
- Foster colleague connections
- Seek out or offer support.

HANDY HINTS

What do people need to build on to become more mentally resilient?

There's a lot of information online telling you how to become more resilient. Below is a list of five things that you can work on today:

1. Recognise what you can and cannot control: even if the situation is not something you can control; you can always control how you react or respond.
2. Build and maintain your support network: studies have shown that social isolation and loneliness are associated with health problems – community or team support helps build resilience.
3. Think like a politician: try to interpret a scenario more favourably. We call this reframing. Almost every situation, regardless of how difficult, can have some potentially positive outcomes. Think about new opportunities that may present themselves or what you can learn (including about yourself). We've all heard the phrases "when one door closes another one opens", or "glass half full".
4. Reflect: think about exposure to previous life stressors. How did you feel? How did you react? What would you do differently if faced with a similar situation? This goes back to John's quote on page 35 about experiential learning.
5. Prepare: if you know you are going into a situation that you know will be uncomfortable, be ok with it. Don't bury your head in the sand, be proactive. If you acknowledge and accept it will be hard or stressful you can quickly find ways to help you cope… remember your raincoat!

CULTURE - THE FOUNDATION, THE FOCUS AND THE PLACE TO START

Some definitions of culture

Chris Dyer:
"The combination of the easily seen ideals like vision statements and values, combined with the harder to see norms, behaviours, languages, beliefs and systems."

Shein:
"A pattern of shared basic assumptions learned by a group as it solved its problems of external adaptation and internal integration."

Flamholtz and Randle:
"Corporate personality."

Deal and Kennedy:
"It's the way things are done around here."

**Communication is the tangible way
of demonstrating culture**

If culture is where the purpose, values and behaviours
sit, then articulating those for employees and sharing
stories that link to them is communication.

If you're looking to be more intentional when it comes
to communicating organisational culture, here are my
five steps to get you started:

1 Find your purpose

Spend time thinking
about the purpose of
your organisation and the
behaviours you want to
see that will deliver that.
What is acceptable and
what isn't acceptable
now that the world of
work is different? What is
needed to enable you to
get things done? Without
this first step, we won't be
able to set an intention
to move forward.

2 Check your channels

Think about the channels
you use to communicate.
Do they reflect where you
are as an organisation and
do they enable you to be
more efficient and more
engaging? What did you
stop and start during
lockdown and what will
you keep or remove?

3 Be action orientated

Focus on outcomes and the acts needed to get there. Listen and respond, don't just listen. And listen in the right way for you – this might be a weekly poll, an annual survey or using technology to go live every month. What's important is that you take action based on what you hear.

4 Mind the say-do gap

Make sure that you do what you say and that your actions and words are closely linked. Trust is a foundational pillar for any culture and there must be trust and respect through the organisation. If you don't know, say you don't know and if you say you will do something by a certain time, do it or explain why it cannot be done.

5 Recognise and reinforce

Recognition and measurement need to be woven into what you do. Make sure you're looking at this with the behaviours in mind and how things will get done. You need to appreciate people and reinforce the good, while also measuring what matters to your organisation.

THE IMPORTANCE OF A PSYCHOLOGICALLY SAFE CULTURE

A topic that has become more prominent is psychological safety. *The Fearless Organization* by Amy Edmondson is grounded in research and insight. It covers everything you need to know about the importance of psychological safety in the workplace and why you need to pay attention to it.

The book outlines what psychological safety is not:

– It is not about personality; or
– Being nice; or
– Another word for trust; or
– About lowering performance standards.

Edmondson defines the difference between trust and safety: "A key difference is that psychological safety is experienced at a group level… Trust on the other hand refers to interactions between two individuals or parties; trust exists in the mind of an individual and pertains to a specific target individual or organisation."

This is an important distinction because it shows how safety links to groups, teams and the organisation as a whole. For me, this supports the importance of communication across groups and teams and the role of relationships in the workplace when it comes to getting things done.

There are huge links to risk, innovation, creativity, problem-solving and more. So, if you're exploring anything around culture, teams and management, you need to be thinking about how psychologically safe people are inside your organisation.

WHY EMPLOYEE ENGAGEMENT NEEDS TO BE MORE THAN JUST CAMPAIGNS AND REWARDS

In *The Art of Resilience* by Ross Edgley, he shares the story of his swim round the UK. There are many aspects to the story that remain with me, and one in particular made me think about how easily we can get things wrong.

Ross talks about an amazing moment where sky writers took to the air to write "100 days" and a love heart in sky as he hit the milestone. While the intention was wonderful and he wasn't ungrateful at all, what he really wanted was… bread. He went on to say it could have been white, brown, granary, any kind – but he wanted bread.

He links this to needs and the different levels suggested by Abraham Maslow's Hierarchy of Needs. The skywriting is an esteem need. It was designed to celebrate him and his accomplishment. It's fairly high up the pyramid, just below self-actualisation, and was done with exactly the right intentions to celebrate the 100-day milestone.

Maslow's hierarchy of needs

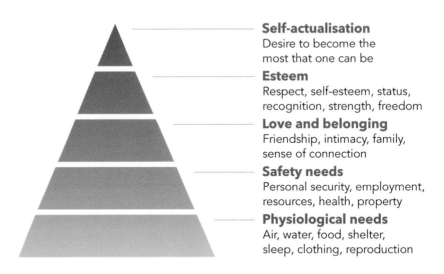

Self-actualisation
Desire to become the
most that one can be

Esteem
Respect, self-esteem, status,
recognition, strength, freedom

Love and belonging
Friendship, intimacy, family,
sense of connection

Safety needs
Personal security, employment,
resources, health, property

Physiological needs
Air, water, food, shelter,
sleep, clothing, reproduction

The reality for Ross, was that he was further down the
pyramid. Much further. In fact, he was at the bottom in
physiological needs where it's all about food, shelter,
warmth and rest.

I talked about this story when I was working with a leader
to help them think about what needs to happen to cope
with the impact of an acquisition. It's so easy for us to think
people are in the right place for recognition and celebration
when the basics just aren't there.

Clients often look at how to adapt internal communication
channels to drive engagement. Or at the broader implications
of business strategy and how it impacts teams and customers.
While others want to find ways to stop "the great resignation"
causing long-term damage to the organisation.

Now is the time to look at all these things through the lens of understanding people. We have to learn more about how we function and respond as human beings for the workplace to thrive. Working together means we have relationships at work and relationships are built on great communication.

To truly engage a workforce, we must understand them. And acknowledge that our brains haven't really changed since we were cave people:

> *"From the 1960s to today, processing power has gone up by about a trillion times. Nothing else that we have has improved at anything near that rate. Cars are roughly twice as fast and almost everything else is negligible. And perhaps most importantly, our human – our physiology, our brains, have evolved not at all."*
>
> Randima (Randy) Fernando, co-founder of the Center for Humane Technology

So, if this is the case (and there are several publications that document this) we have to start with what our brain is actually designed to do and that's keeping us safe. When we don't feel secure or our brain can't predict what is going to happen, it stops us from doing things and elicits a threat response in our bodies (stress, worry, anxiety). Our brain will also fill in the blanks by making up stories that enable us to predict – even if those stories are false.

Let's think about that for a moment and what that means for work and the culture of the organisations we work with.

In a world that is currently changing at pace, with lots of unknowns and continuing concerns around public health and safety, our brains are in overdrive trying to make sense of it all.

We create a campaign to drive engagement. We create a campaign to help people understand why working here is great. We ignore the real issues. We ignore the real challenges they are facing. We ignore the things that help them feel safe and enable them to predict.

If you want to drive real, sustainable change inside your organisation that engages teams and helps people thrive, take the time to reflect on how people really feel right now. Take a moment to think about whether your messages are going to help people achieve some stability and remove the worry that blocks progress and productivity.

CULTURE AND ITS IMPACT ON DIVERSITY, INCLUSION, EQUITY AND BELONGING

Culture is such a broad topic that it covers almost every other section in this book. Importantly it is how things get done and that means it is inherently linked to diversity, inclusion, equity and belonging as well as hybrid working.

The importance of diversity, inclusion and belonging has risen but that importance has ebbed and flowed over the course of the last two years.

There is a need to focus more on being human in the workplace. To really consider what this means for work and culture.

We are human. We are people. If we can stop dehumanizing individuals and groups and recognise that we are all human beings, it would be a foundational shift in the systemic issues that plague our society. We are easily flippant. We are quickly judgmental. We aren't purposeful enough and we aren't always aware of our impact on others.

What is being done to ensure people belong? How are processes changing to ensure fairness and equity across the organisation? How much are we considering the individual rather than the group.

There are a lot of questions for everyone at work around this area of culture – it's why it is a broad topic and it's why we have to look at the whole employee experience, the processes and the training needs for everyone we work with.

*Be Inspired

Safety at work
The importance of psychological safety in organisations has been a conversation for a few years.

The Fearless Organisation by Amy Edmondson is packed with references to other research and clear theory behind why psychological safety is the foundation for organisations. There are references to how it differs to trust and the importance of how "unseen" it is when someone doesn't feel safe enough to speak up.

Freedom in a Framework
It might be a few years old, but I have enjoyed reading *The Trust Factor* by Paul J Zak. In the book, Paul references "Freedom in a Framework" and it's one that I first heard from my Clubhouse co-moderator, Jim Egan.

As conversations around hybrid working continue, this is a great phrase to keep top of mind. I have been speaking at online events and on podcasts about this topic and keeping it simple is one of the best pieces of advice I can offer.

If you want to hear more about some of my thoughts on hybrid working you can check out the CIPR *Engage* podcast episode three, where I interview three panellists about the topic and what it really means for organisations.

The series everyone was talking about
Schitts Creek – it was the series of 2020 that everyone around me was talking about. We stretched it out as much as we could and we finished it with an extra behind-the-scenes episode called "Best Wishes, warmest regards".

Why is it inspiring? It shares insights into why the show is so successful from a character depth perspective and, when you explore the inclusivity side of the show and how it has impacted the lives of those in the LGBTQ+ community, you realise just how well written, directed and produced it was.

COMMUNICATION IS CULTURE

How you communicate inside an organisation is the tangible way of demonstrating culture. The culture is seen through the channels you use, the innovation of those channels, the tone of voice that is used and the role of employees in communication.

Culture and communication are constantly entwined inside organisations. If culture is where the purpose, values and behaviours sit, then articulating those for employees and sharing stories that link to them is communication.

How culture is seen through communication

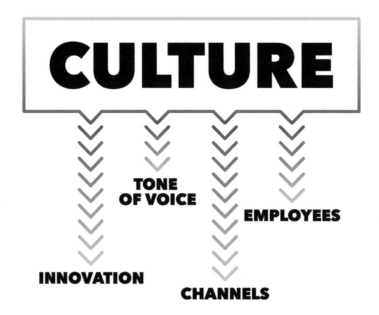

Source: Influential Internal Communication by Jenni Field

LEADERSHIP

To lead isn't to change.

As a leader you should inspire, challenge and demonstrate a vision that people can follow. This doesn't necessarily mean you need to change everything. The defining trait for leaders shouldn't be their ability to transform: doing what you do well, focusing on the basics and becoming an impactful communicator is vital.

We need to get comfortable being uncomfortable

As leaders, there's a need to make decisions, have difficult conversations and be accountable. Leading a team or an organisation is not always easy so having a strong team around you, listening to the right people and investing in yourself is important. When it comes to leading organisations we have to remember that there is now a barrier between the customer or the client and the people inside the organisation - this is the brand.

If we look back in history and the transactions that used to happen - a cart from a carpenter in exchange for other goods or services - we can see that we used to buy things directly from the person who made them.

Now, we buy things from brands and from bigger organisations. In turn, this creates distance between the customer and the people inside the organisation.

That distance that emerges between an individual and the product or service leads us to be removed from consequence. As a leader, it's easy to be distant from the impact of the organisation.

There are always consequences from actions. As decision makers, there will always be consequences. There will always be compromise needed and there will always be a need to be accountable.

This is something we have to get comfortable with and it links back to our ability to be genuine, to know our purpose and to know our values.

*Be Inspired

Books

One of my favourite book titles is: *Your Oxygen Mask First* by Kevin N Lawrence. The book explains the habits that high achievers can develop to survive and thrive in leadership. This is exactly the approach that's needed – look after yourself first.

Being brave or being daring is a leadership approach pioneered by Brené Brown. Her books, podcast and Netflix programme are all worth checking out if this is an area of interest too.

Elvin Turner is an innovation expert and author of *Be Less Zombie: How great companies create dynamic innovation, fearless leadership and passionate people* talks about the importance of trust in leadership. When discussing the role of innovation and leadership, Turner shared his views on the importance of trust:

> *"Building trust means creating confident expectations about how you'll behave. Trust is the level of confidence that I have in what you'll do and how you'll do it. That means it's both a matter of capability and character. Organisations that can trust their people to make the right decisions and get things done, move faster and innovate better. Trust is a performance game-changer, but often we avoid the conversations that build it because they feel too personal or confrontational."*

TV

The Apple TV series, *Ted Lasso*, starring Jason Sudeikis as a college football coach from Kansas hired to coach the fictional Richmond FC is a masterclass in leadership.

It is a great watch in terms of positivity, different styles of leadership, and getting to know people. There's so much to take away from this – the writing and casting are brilliant, but the importance of building human connections and spending time getting to know people more is a constant thread. Ted's approach is upbeat and leads with kindness; he sees the good in everybody.

The Bold Type on Netflix is four seasons following three female friends working at a fashion magazine in America.

Inspired by the life of former *Cosmopolitan* editor-in-chief Joanna Coles, who also serves as executive producer, the seasons take you on a journey of their careers and personal lives.

Melora Hardin is brilliant as the editor-in-chief Jacqueline Carlyle – this character could easily have been hard and cold but instead she is warm, kind and full of empathy, with a fierceness to her that commands respect.

Reports

For those keen to read something more research based or academic, *Leadership's Digital Transformation from MIT Sloan Management Review* is the one to explore.

It covers a breadth of topics but all focused on leadership in the digital era. The report shares findings from a study, and it proves the importance of purpose and the value of diversity in teams. It explores the concept of context collapse – how social media has flattened multiple audiences into one – and how this has been heightened by the pandemic.

THE IMPORTANCE OF ACCOUNTABILITY

I can't stress enough the importance of accountability, especially when it comes to productivity, leadership skills and resilience.

A podcast episode from Brené Brown, *Unlocking Us: Words, Actions, Dehumanisation and Accountability*, recorded shortly after the January 2021 Capitol riots, reinforced why it's accountability we need to focus on when it comes to change.

She talks about how...

"shame undermines accountability and shame corrodes empathy."

As she explores dehumanisation she references the work of Michelle Maiese, Associate Professor of Philosophy at Emmanuel College who defines dehumanisation as...

"the psychological process of demonising the enemy making them less than human and hence not worthy of humane treatment."

All of this got me thinking even more about psychological safety in the workplace and how we can ensure we work in diverse and inclusive spaces that focus more on action, the human experience at work and trust.

HANDY HINTS

Six skills to master to be a better leader

1. Compassion

This feels like something leaders are often told they don't need, but research shows that vulnerability and courage go hand in hand. And with that, comes compassion.

We're all human and showing some of that in the workplace leads to more genuine relationships and builds trust. Part of this involves making time to talk to people and focus on the individual completely.

2. Look after yourself

You're a key player and it's essential to focus on your health, wellbeing and build mental resilience to be able to lead others effectively.

Developing routine practices that manage your time and attention can help avoid burnout. Whether it's a 30-minutes yoga or workout session in the morning, a brisk walk at lunchtime or stopping to take three deep breaths – make time for you, every day.

3. Respect

This works both ways. It works every way. Respect must be given to everyone regardless of hierarchy. For some this comes naturally and for others it feels alien.

Respect the time and expertise of others; you hired them for a reason.

4. Time v. attention management

As a leader it's easy to be pulled in lots of directions! Multitasking increases the time it takes to complete a task by 40%, and the optimal time for you to focus is around 52 minutes with a 17-minute break.

You need to focus your attention, not your time. The meetings and conversations are needed, so focus your attention on what will make a difference and add value.

5. Self-awareness

Knowing your limits is a huge strength in leadership. It's hard to show vulnerability and let someone know you need assistance. Find your trusted circle and use them to help you navigate your growth.

No one expects you to do this alone, so make sure you know when and how to ask for help if you feel a little lost. This isn't a weakness; it's an awareness that you can't possibly know everything – that's why you hired a diverse and talented team, right? You can reap huge rewards by asking for help.

"It's easy to work through a list of questions and make a note of the answers. But if you're actively listening, you're taking the person on a journey to help them work their way to the core of the issue. This isn't an easy skill to develop and it takes time to master. It's worth investing that time because then you're listening to understand, not just to respond."

6. Listening

Listening to those around you is a hugely important skill for leaders. A leader's response when someone is sharing or talking has more weight than a peer. Remember that how you show you're actively listening is equally important.

How leaders can influence people around them

1. Be genuine
You have to be you. Not someone you think people want you to be. This will allow you to be authentic and real with those around you. It not only builds trust, it helps you build proper relationships.

2. Lead with empathy
Listen first. Listen to understand, not reply. Really listen. Listen to the words people use, how they say them and pay attention to them – be present in the conversation. Take a servant-leadership approach and ask "how can I help?"

3. Be intentional
Be intentional with your time and align it to your goals. When you have a clear direction, others will follow.

4. Purpose
This isn't necessarily about you having a huge purpose, but consultant, Simon Farrell, talks about organisations being purposeful or purpose-led, and this is a great approach to explore. Consider motivation and the link between purpose, autonomy and mastery. You will struggle to influence if your only reason for doing something is financial reward.

5. Be the expert
Invest in yourself. You need the right skills to be able to advise others and being an expert in your field will create trust.

6. Demonstrate value and integrity
Ask the question – what does value mean to you in terms of what I do? The answer will help you shape how you talk about what you do. If you say you're going to do something, do it: integrity is so important for trust and, as a result, leadership and influence.

UNDERSTANDING OURSELVES, BEING BUSY AND HOW TO STAY FOCUSED

Productivity:
How efficient we are.

Too busy:
When we use busy as an excuse or a reason for not doing something it is actually when we are prioritising other things.

Time management:
It's not about how we spend our time, it's about how we focus our attention.

Being productive isn't about being at home

There are a lot of reports out there about how productive people are when they work from home. There is a report to support any argument but most of the research is based on opinion. We will always think we are better than we are or that we will make better choices than we will.

In a podcast episode from *The Diary of a CEO*, hosted by Stephen Bartlett, he interviewed retail consultant and broadcaster, Mary Portas. Part of their conversation turns to remote work and the importance of the office. Mary says:

> *"We have two days where we say we want everybody in... Even when I go in, and I will see them all, and we all have laugh, and we'll talk about stuff that's not even in the work world. But those nuggets, those little messages, those little nuances that happen are what makes us human..."*

When I shared that clip on social media, I wasn't expecting the barrage of comments from people who seemed quite angry about the prospect of returning to the office.

The comments and discussion made me want to find data into the impact of working from home (WFH) on productivity. Lots of the remarks around returning to the office stem from a belief that we get more done without a commute. This is when I read the IZA Institute of Labor Economics report *Work from Home & Productivity: Evidence from Personnel & Analytics Data on IT Professionals*, published in May 2021. The key takeaway worth noting is that working from home reduces productivity by 20%.

The research was carried out using data and metrics from computer usage and work time rather than people's opinions. It also compared data from before the boom in WFH so we can see the change that happened.

The paper includes insights from other research from their literature review, which helps us understand the need for more research in this area – but also supports some of the findings of this paper too:

"The UK Household Longitudinal Survey indicated that employees who work from home believe that they are about as productive as they were in the office (Etheridge et al., 2020). Those who did perceive declines in productivity also experienced lower levels of well-being from WFH. Bellmann and Hübler (2020) find that working remotely has no long-run effect on work-life balance, and that a switch to WFH increases job satisfaction only temporarily."

This discussion paper is based on research that was carried out with 10,000 skilled workers. They were IT professionals, all with degrees and all based in an Asian country. This is important to note as the researcher discusses some cultural nuances in the findings when it comes to gender.

There is a lot in the findings but here are the top five things I took from the report:

1 Evidence indicates that employees worked longer but less productively, with output remaining about the same. People are less productive because they still aim to reach the same output or goals, they just work longer to be able to achieve that level of output.

2 Employees spend more time in meetings or on calls and have less "focus time" (i.e., time uninterrupted by meetings or calls to focus on completing tasks). The increased time spent in meetings, and its persistence after the initial WFH transition phase, suggest substantial and ongoing coordination costs with WFH. This negatively impacts time available to work in a productive manner.

3 WFH has a detrimental impact on communication, collaboration and innovation.

4 The patterns highlight a detrimental impact of WFH on networking. Employees have fewer contacts with different individuals and organisational units both inside and outside the company. They also have fewer one-to-one meetings with superiors and receive less coaching. These lost opportunities to network may help explain why WFH lowers productivity. It is also likely that they slow employee development, though that is beyond the research paper.

5 WFH induced a significant shift in working patterns. Employees work more, including after regular office hours, but have less uninterrupted time to focus on task completion as they spend more time in meetings. They network less and spend less time being evaluated, trained and coached. It further showed that these reductions, especially in focus hours and networking, are detrimental to productivity.

Ultimately – this is part of the conclusion in the report and nicely summarises why it is a risk for communication, innovation, and collaboration:

> *"It is likely that working from home resulted in a decline in intangibles that are valuable to the employee and company. Increased coordination costs may mean that teams and other working relationships suffered. Employees spent less time networking with each other and people outside the company. That would lead to a loss of social capital if this continued. More subtly, when people work in the same location, they experience unplanned interactions. That can lead to new working relationships and 'productive accidents' that spur innovation."*

As Mary Portas says, if we take away these unscheduled opportunities to connect: "we take what it is to be human."

SET BOUNDARIES TO INCREASE YOUR PRODUCTIVITY

Being productive and focused is connected with impactful communication skills. Managing your time links to managing relationships and setting boundaries with those at work. Sometimes these conversations are difficult to have, but if we continue to avoid them it makes work a very challenging place.

Where time management falls down:
- It is not a one-size-fits-all, which time management training can often prescribe
- There has to be solutions that suit your work, your role and your life. Trying to squeeze into something else won't work and will lead to further issues
- Being realistic is key. No one is productive all the time. In fact, that's not good for you at all as the brain needs time to be quiet. Time management training can often lead you feeling more overwhelmed than when you walked in.

I will always remember someone in my team returning from training and declaring they were only going to check emails once in the morning and once in the evening as a result. When you are running a busy internal communication function in an organisation that operates for customers 24/7 that is just never going to work.

So, when I talk about productivity and boundaries, I'm talking about the boundaries for you and your time but importantly, your attention and focus.

We are easily interrupted. We have notifications pinging on phones and laptops that take us away from what we are doing. These interruptions impact our ability to stay focused. In fact, it can take up to 23 minutes to recover from them.

Be clear about how you work:

- Define the hours you are available for meetings
- Use your out-of-office email message to manage expectations
- Question why you're being invited to meetings so you know your role and purpose
- Be consistent and fair to everyone
- Turn off notifications
- Build in rewards when you complete a task.

COMPARISON IS THE THIEF OF JOY, AND COMPARING BUSYNESS IS THE WORST THING YOU CAN DO

In the last year we have seen an increased competitive nature coming through in conversations about how busy we are. Our need to be busier than someone else or another team is leading to friction and a lack of respect in the workplace.

What is competitive busyness?

It can happen in groups, teams or across organisations: "I can't make that meeting I'm too busy this week", or "They have no idea how busy we are in this team, and they keep asking for more."

It can come from a feeling that you are doing so much more and working so much harder than those around you, leading to feeling angry and irritated by those who you perceive are not working as hard.

Firstly, being busy is not an award you want to win. It's not something to strive for and being too busy to do anything isn't good for you or those you work with. It's why I coach people to focus on the goals for them and the activities that support those.

And secondly, this is all linked to our need to compare ourselves to others. Comparison is the thief of joy and comparing how much you're doing against someone else doesn't help you at all. If anything, it can lead to a lot of negative thinking and self-sabotage.

THE SCIENCE BIT...

We are all individual. This means that some of the things society imposes on us don't work for everyone. It's why some people love a night shift and others can't think of anything worse. When we consider that, for many, jobs have been nine to five, the pandemic changed that. Time and how we spend it was thrown into complete chaos.

There is some science here that can help us understand this a bit more and it's important for us to do this when it comes to getting the best from ourselves; circadian rhythms and zeitgebers.

Circadian rhythm is the body's built-in clock. It works in 24-hour cycles and is responsible for regulating your biological rhythms, such as sleep, mood, or cognitive performance.

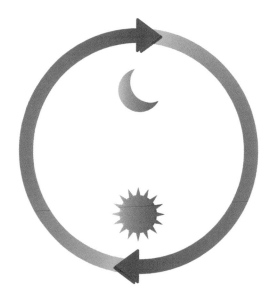

Jurgen Aschoff, a German physician, found that our circadian rhythm is synchronised to the earth's 24-hour light cycle and the cues that we get from the earth like light and dark – these are zeitgebers. They are the cues that keep us functioning on a regular schedule.

Societally imposed timings like the working day, times to eat or school days are zeitgbers. Zeitgebers are intrinsically linked to our circadian rhythm.

To keep the circadian rhythm running as it should our bodies rely on zeitgebers.

The pandemic and enforced changes to work and lives meant that our societally imposed zeitgebers were gone. In turn, this impacted our circadian rhythm. And that impacts our mood, our ability to sleep and our cognitive function. It's why many struggled to focus, struggled with any sort of routine and why moods kept changing.

Your circadian rhythm is individual to you. Which means that when the societally imposed zeitgebers are gone, you are likely to be adjusting to your natural rhythm. And it might not match the old ways of an office job that was nine to five. We need to acknowledge and understand ourselves so we can put our own zeitgebers in place to help us function.

We are all individual and taking the time to work out our rhythm without the societal timetable we have had imposed on us for hundreds of years will take time.

*Be Inspired

Beating procrastination and focusing your attention

5, 4, 3, 2, 1 move! Mel Robbins' book *The 5 Second Rule* (no, it's not about how long you can leave food on the floor). If you're looking for a technique to beat procrastination and get out of your own head, this is the book for you. Two things that stood out for me:

1. I use the tool to get moving. It helps me get my walks in every day
2. It's not about the outcome. It's not about what happens when I do the thing after I countdown. It's about the fact I am moving forward towards my goals. This is the most powerful thing I have taken away from the book.

How to Thrive in a World of Too Much by Tony Crabbe is another great book. Packed with insights and research into how we work, it will help you think about the importance of focusing your attention and the need to make the world around you a bit quieter.

For a quick listen, grab episode three of *Redefining Communications with Jenni Field* podcast – it's 15 minutes of how to go from chaos to calm through improving your attention management.

HANDY HINTS

What can you do to remove competitive busyness?

1. Open discussion: have conversations about workload and current challenges to getting the work done
2. Identify boundaries: explore how the individuals and teams have set boundaries with each other
3. Pinpoint dependencies: encourage conversations about the impact of the ask. How does it alter time, cost or resource?
4. Support managers: give them the skills to have these (sometimes difficult) conversations with their teams
5. Call out negative commentary: if people start talking about how they are busier or how another team clearly isn't busy – lean into it to stop it.

There are lots of things you can do to work on the communication and relationships across teams in your organisation but remembering that there is a relationship there to manage and build on is an important acknowledgment.

Focusing your attention

Three things to try to get your attention focused on the task:

1. Eat the frog: a metaphor for the worst thing you need to do. Possibly the biggest task of the day or the thing you've been putting off. Get it done early and there is nothing worse you will do that day!
2. Use timers: 30 minutes is a good timer for a task. Set it for when you need to write a report, clear emails, write a presentation. Whatever it is, set yourself a time to help you stay focused.
3. The rule of five things: never have more than five things on your to-do list in a day. It can be one big thing and four small or two medium and three small. Five things is the best amount when you will have interruptions and meetings in the day too. If your day is full of meetings – that's all you can do!

WHAT IS THE FIELD MODEL™?

Understand
Diagnose
Fix

The Field Model™

The Field Model™ came from a conversation about how I describe what I do. Over the years the need to be mindful, explore other perspectives and manage emotional reactions has led to better conversations and quicker problem solving.

When I describe what I do I don't describe the activities, I describe the fact that I can bring calm to the chaos inside the organisation. The Field Model codifies what naturally happens when you start to explore why things are happening.

Often when I'm approached by a potential client it's because they have a pressing issue. They understand the immediate effect that the issue is having on the business and its employees. And there may even have been previous attempts to solve those issues. However, these attempts are frequently short-term fixes. This is because, without understanding and dealing with the root cause, real change can't happen.

If we use a medical analogy, we're just dealing with the symptoms. If I have a headache, I might not be able to focus as well, so my first thought is to take a painkiller. But if I keep getting headaches, then I need to look at what is causing it – is it tension, am I getting enough sleep, do I need to correct my posture, should I get my eyes tested – or is it a combination of all these factors?

In organisations this presents as a feeling of chaos and, particularly if it's toxic chaos, it can be damaging. The 'headache' could be a stressed workforce, high attrition, misaligned functions after an acquisition, absenteeism, teams not working together well, and so on.

A wellbeing campaign or new development programme might make things better for a bit, but soon (normally around two years in fact) old issues start to trickle back in. So, we must understand there is a problem, diagnose why it exists and fix it.

Here's an overview of the three elements to The Field Model: Understand – Diagnose – Fix.

UNDERSTAND

We often understand something is wrong. We might not know why but we know we need to do something. It might be because people are leaving, people are off with stress, there has been significant change in the organisation through growth, M&A, crisis – whatever it is we know something isn't right.

This is the first step – we understand the symptoms. It can be the most ambiguous part because we often, incorrectly, wrap up understand and diagnose together. Listening and understanding every facet of the issue will help us explore why there's a need to change.

DIAGNOSE

We must diagnose the cause of the symptoms – the why? There will be reasons for things not being right, and we need to uncover what's really going on. If you fix the symptoms you won't be fixing things for the long term.

Diagnosing takes time but it starts with listening for patterns in language and feelings. Diagnosis can take many forms; from interviews, surveys, focus groups to one-to-one sessions with leadership.

The right way to diagnose depends on your situation, organisation and budget. The conversations we have at this stage need to be with an open mind, without any pre-conceived ideas of what the solution might be.

"The tangible output of The Field Model is a comprehensive report but talking through the findings added real value. With a direct and outcome-focused approach, Jenni offered guidance and strategic direction to get us to a better place. Insightful and with a natural instinct that is right, Jenni is also not afraid to tell it as it is!"

Ben Reynolds, Managing Director of Gallagher's Employee Experience and Communication division

FIX

Now we can fix the real issues. This is where you need to be comfortable getting uncomfortable. It will require aspects of vulnerability, bravery, courage and listening to others.

It can take anything from a few months to a few years, but you are fixing the things that are at the root cause of the symptoms. Often, the fix is about refocusing your time and energy into a different place and we work with organisations to provide a clear plan to take forward.

What does fix look like? How can communication cover it all?

Communication is the fundamental component, the golden thread, that runs through everything. It is representative of culture, it is the articulation of the strategy, and it's what we need to function as a group or community. So yes, communication covers it all.

Depending on the issue there are several ways the fix takes place. A task force can be set up, you can opt for "on-site fix" that requires someone outside the organisation being in it for a period of time to move it forward (or turn it upside down for a while).

It's important to mention that The Field Model isn't finite; you don't work through each stage and then stop. You have to be part of the circle. There might be different reasons for using The Field Model inside your organisation over time and what it uncovers might lead to the need for further insight.

The Field Model allows you to structure your thinking, your approach and your timescales to deal with the issues that will allow you to carry on running the organisation. Things don't have to stop while this is carried out, but things will need to be agile and people will need to be open to the change.

It can be applied to teams, organisations, communication functions and more.

· ·

"Our business was experiencing a mass of chaos from industry changes, the fallout of COVID-19 and restructuring programmes. It was making communications complex, unfocused and unorganised. Through applying The Field Model™ with Jenni, we were able to pinpoint and understand areas we could make improvements.

Working with Jenni has been a fantastic experience. Not only is she an expert, but she is also friendly and down to earth. We can't thank her enough for her support."

Karen McCann, Internal Communications Senior Manager, Greater Anglia

AND FINALLY...

WHAT ARE THE THEMES FOR THE YEARS AHEAD?

As we look forward there are lots of things on the agenda for organisations and communication teams. Environment, social and governance (ESG), the departure from the EU for the UK, the repercussions of the global pandemic are just three things that come to mind when we look forward.

For the internal communicator, the list of things to focus on continues to grow. At the October 2021 unconference event called The Big Yak, over 100 internal communication professionals identified topics they wanted to discuss on the day:

– Hybrid working
– Measurement
– Women's safety
– Behavioural science
– Time management, planning and prioritisation
– Personal brand
– Future skills
– Channel strategy
– Line managers
– Frontline worker communication
– Engagement in tech
– Employee experience

- Wellbeing
- Stakeholder mapping/targeting
- Hybrid events
- How to stay relevant
- Leadership after COVID-19
- Purpose
- Setting up/developing an internal comms team
- Diversity and inclusion.

When it comes to looking forward, the focus for organisations is likely to continue to be trust and transparency, sustainability, and technology. Big topics that will require insight, conversation and strategic thinking to deliver against organisational goals.

Keep the conversation going
Connect with Redefining Communications
and Jenni Field:

Twitter
@redefiningcomms
@mrsjennifield

Instagram
@jennifield

LinkedIn
Search for Jenni Field and Redefining Communications

Email the team
info@redefiningcomms.com

Find out more about us
www.redefiningcomms.com

Topical talk
Launched in October 2021, the *Redefining
Communications with Jenni Field* podcast tackles
the latest business topics causing chaos within
organisations and offers helpful tips. Each 15-minute
jam-packed episode has proved a resounding
success. Listen wherever you find your podcasts.

FURTHER READING

The 5 Second Rule by Mel Robbins

The Algebra of Purpose LinkedIn article by Simon Farrell

Ambiguity, resilience, and the Stockdale Paradox blog by Redefining Communications

The Art of Resilience by Ross Edgley

Be Less Zombie: How great companies create dynamic innovation, fearless leadership and passionate people by Elvin Turner

Best Wishes, Warmest Regards: A Schitt's Creek Farewell on Netflix

The Bionic Business report by Simply Communicate

The Bold Type series on Netflix

Brené Brown books, podcasts and Netflix documentary called *The Call to Courage*

Brené Brown interview with Jason Sudeikis and Brendan Hunt on *Ted Lasso* series.

Burnout – Solve Your Stress Cycle by Emily and Amelia Nagoski

Burnout and How to Complete the Stress Cycle Brené Brown podcast with Emily and Amelia Nagoski

Calm Edged Rebels podcast

Chaos to Calm: Hybrid Working podcast by Redefining Communications with Jenni Field

Chaos to Calm: Staying focused podcast by Redefining Communications with Jenni Field

The Diary of a CEO podcast interview by Stephen Bartlett with Mary Portas

Engage: Hybrid Working podcast by the Chartered Institute of Public Relations (CIPR)

The Fearless Organization by Amy Edmondson

Five ways to stay productive and focused download via the Redefining Communications website

Forbes: Why Resilience Is Necessary As A Leader by Amy Modglin (CEO, Modglin Leadership Solutions)

Harvard Business Review: America's Loneliest Workers

Hierarchy of Needs: A Theory of Human Motivation by Abraham H. Maslow

How to Humour Your Stress TED Talk by Loretta LaRoche

How to say no: creating balance and boundaries podcast by Calm Edged Rebels Series 2, Episode 3

How to Thrive in a World of Too Much by Tony Crabbe

Influence publication by the Chartered Institute of Public Relations (CIPR)

Influential Internal Communication by Jenni Field (published by Kogan Page)

Keep calm: fix organisational chaos, streamline communication and drive engagement by Jenni Field for the International Association of Business Communicators (IABC)

Leadership's Digital Transformation report from MIT Sloan Management Review

Life Under Fire by Jason Fox

Line of Sight research by Redefining Communications

The Long-Distance Leader by Kevin Eikenberry and Wayne Turmel

Meditations by Marcus Aurelius

Mistakes Were Made (but not by me) by Carol Tavris and Elliot Aronson

Notes on a Nervous Planet by Matt Haig

The Obstacle is the Way by Ryan Holiday

Psychology Today The Queen's Gambit: A Story of Psychological Resiliency by Mariana Bockarova, Ph.D.

The Queen's Gambit Netflix series

Rebel Ideas by Matthew Syed

Remote Work by Chris Dyer and Kim Shepherd

The Science of Fear: How the Culture of Fear Manipulations Your Brain by Daniel Gardner

The Social Dilemma documentary on Netflix

Spotting burnout: seven ways to solve your stress cycle blog by Redefining Communications

Staying focused and being productive podcast by Calm Edged Rebels Series 1, Episode 2

Ted Lasso on Apple TV

The Trust Factor by Paul J Zak

UK Household Longitudinal Survey by Understanding Society

Unlocking Us: Words, Actions, Dehumanisation and Accountability podcast by Brené Brown

What is Mental Resilience blog by John Humphreys on Redefining Communications website

Will hybrid working ever work? research by *Management Today* partnered with Hays

Work from Home & Productivity: Evidence from Personnel & Analytics Data on IT Professionals report by the IZA Institute of Labor Economics

Worldwide Digital Transformation 2021 Predictions by IDC FutureScape

Your Oxygen Mask First by Kevin N. Lawrence

ACKNOWLEDGEMENTS AND THANKS

- Adam Mitchinson for the creative design and bringing the words to life
- Adam Larsson for suggesting the title of this book
- Chloe Michel for all her copywriting support over the last few years
- Jacqui Batten for the editing and the creative thinking
- Jim Egan, Scott McInnes and AnnMarie Phillips for the Clubhouse conversations that have inspired so much of my thinking
- John Humphreys for the mental resilience content we share.

Printed in Great Britain
by Amazon

81133401R00058